THE MONTH BY MONTH TREASURE BOX

Crafty Things To Do With Young Children

by
Sally Patrick
Vicky Schwartz
Pat LoPresti

Incentive Publications, Inc.
Nashville, Tennessee

Dedicated to the
Preschool PTA
Lexington, MA

Illustrated by Gayle Seaberg Harvey
Edited by Jennifer Goodman and Sally Sharpe
Cover by Susan Eaddy

Library of Congress Catalog Card Number 86-82599
ISBN 0-86530-124-7

TABLE OF CONTENTS

FOREWORD

We bring you this book to share activities that we have enjoyed doing with our own preschoolers as well as with others. The activities have worked for us with groups ranging in size from ten to over a hundred children and adults. These projects help develop a child's attention span, as well as encourage creativity and enrich the imagination.

We present an easy-to-use format, organized by month, to take you through the year. The crafts are for two and three-year-olds to do with your assistance. However, you will find that older preschoolers enjoy them just as much. These projects are open-ended. You can modify them, enlarge them, or simplify them; but, most of all, you can have fun with them. You will become a collector of discarded milk cartons, a connoisseur of clay, and a museum "curator" for the art your preschooler will produce. We hope you will enjoy these experiences as much as we have.

INTRODUCTION

You'll find these shortcuts to be very helpful, whether you are working with your own child at home or with a large group of children.

COLORING Markers produce brighter colors than crayons and are easier for young crafters to use.

GLUING A pair of cups cut from an egg carton makes a fine glue holder. Pour a little white glue in the cups and use a cotton swab as an applicator.

KEEPING CLEAN A layer of newspaper on the table makes cleaning up easier if the project is a particularly messy one. The floor is also a good place to work. An adult's old T-shirt makes a terrific smock.

STRINGING For projects involving stringing or weaving, cut a length of yarn and dip an inch or so of one end in white glue. Allow the yarn to dry and you have a "needle."

PAINTING AND PRINTING Baby food jars and small milk cartons are excellent paint holders. For printing, pour a small amount of diluted tempera paint over a paper towel folded in half in a Styrofoam vegetable tray.

SUPPLIES Assemble a box of frequently used craft supplies, your "treasure box." Fill another box with cleanup materials. Below are useful items to include in each box.

CLEANUP BOX

dishpan
sponges
baby shampoo
paper towels

TREASURE BOX

glue holders made
    from egg cartons
white glue
newsprint
construction paper
markers and crayons
scissors

cotton swabs
craft sticks
paintbrushes
tempera paint
stapler and staples
yarn or string
tape: clear and
    masking

LEAD TIME Collecting materials for some projects requires time. It might take you several weeks to acquire enough egg cartons, pine cones, Styrofoam vegetable trays, coffee cans or cardboard tubes for a planned activity. Notify your group by sending a list of desired "throwaways" home with each crafter or by including a list in your newsletter.

CRAFTER'S LAW The more material you distribute, the more will be used. Extra material could be put on a separate table accessible to adults.

SET UP Arrange materials according to projects. Distribute paper, markers and scissors to each craft area; then, put out those items needed for the first project.

USE YOUR COMMUNITY Invite your local fire and/or police department to visit your group. Include one of the appropriate projects on that day.

LOCATION If you belong to a PTA, your local school system may make space available to you on a regular basis. Other possible locations are libraries, town halls, churches, and community organizations.

TRY IT OUT Try out your planned activity with a child at least a day in advance.

ASSEMBLE MATERIALS From the "treasure box," take out project tools for the day's activities. Bring along any supplementary materials needed for those specific projects.

CRAFTING Greet your crafters and explain the project. After 15 or 20 minutes, you may want to go on to another project, serve a snack, or simply clean up.

CLEANUP Collect from each craft area scissors, markers, and all throwaways. Take a clean, wet sponge to each table and delegate the job to someone. Thank your helpers!

TOYS Keep a box of safe, durable toys for younger siblings, for those speedy crafters who race through their projects, or for children who wish to take a break.

JANUARY

MODELING CLAY

Modeling clay provides hours of fun and a nice break from more active play. Children may want to mold their clay into shapes or roll it flat and cut out shapes with cookie cutters. With a play stove and dishes, children can "boil" a pan of peas or "bake" a pizza. You may want to keep a separate box of plastic or old utensils, cookie cutters and other items for your children to use with modeling clay.

YOU WILL NEED:
1/2 cup salt
2 tsp. cream of tartar
1 cup water
1 tbs. cooking oil
2 cups flour
food coloring

Combine ingredients and stir constantly over medium heat for five minutes or until stiff. Tinting the water beforehand with food coloring will give a better distribution of color. Cool thoroughly before using. Store modeling clay in a covered plastic container or plastic bag.

# JANUARY

BIRD FEEDERS

CEREAL ON A STRING FEEDER

YOU WILL NEED:
  doughnut-shaped cereal
    (Cheerios)™
  string or yarn

Children can make bird feeders by threading cereal on yarn or string. After tying the ends together, they can hang the feeder from a special tree branch.

WOOD BLOCK FEEDER

YOU WILL NEED:
  small block of wood
  2 to 3-inch nail
  hammer
  eye screw
  yarn or string
  doughnut

Help children hammer the nail partially into the wooden block. The eye screw is added to the top. Children can thread the eye screw with the string and then place a doughnut on the nail. Hung on a chosen branch, this feeder is definitely for the birds!

PINE CONE FEEDER

YOU WILL NEED:
  pine cone
  yarn or string
  peanut butter (thinned with
      vegetable oil, so the birds
      won't get sick)
  craft stick
  paper plate
  birdseed

Assist children in tying string on
the wider end of the pine cone to
make a hanger. Children spread
the peanut butter on the pine
cones with craft sticks and then roll
the gooey cones in the birdseed.
Holding the cones over paper
plates while carrying them outside
is a good idea!

BERRY BASKET FEEDER

YOU WILL NEED:
  plastic berry basket
  string
  bread
  peanut butter
  birdseed
  craft stick

Using a craft stick, children spread
peanut butter on both sides of a
piece of bread. After pressing the
bread into birdseed, they put the
bread in their baskets. Assist them
in joining opposite sides of their
baskets and in fastening them with
string. Allow enough string for
hanging the feeder.

JANUARY

VEST

YOU WILL NEED:
   large brown paper bag
   scissors
   markers, crayons, or paint

Open the bag. Remove one narrow side and the bottom. Trim the corners to make a curved vest front. Add armholes on each side about two inches below the neckline. Children may want to fringe the vest with single cuts around the edges. A sheriff's badge can be added to the front of the vest. Using markers, crayons, or paint, children can decorate their vests.

SADDLE BAG

YOU WILL NEED:
   a circular piece of lightweight
      cloth, 7 to 8 inches in diameter
   yarn, 18 inches long with tip
      dipped in glue and dried to form
      a "needle"
   hole punch or scissors

Approximately one inch from the edge, evenly space holes around the cloth circle. Children sew their saddle bags by lacing yarn through the holes. Assist them in tying the ends of the yarn together and drawing the yarn to close the bag.

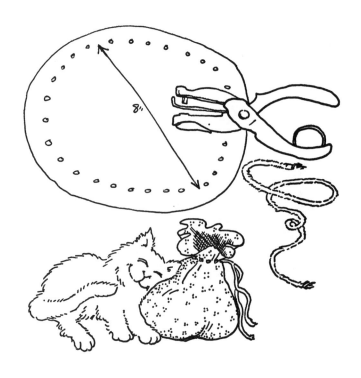

JANUARY ❄

HOBBY HORSE

YOU WILL NEED:
- sturdy, long cardboard tube such as gift-wrap insert
- paper lunch bag
- construction paper
- scissors
- markers
- masking tape
- newspaper

Children crumple newspaper and stuff paper bags three-quarters full. The bottom of the bag will be the horse's nose and mouth. Children insert two to three inches of the tube in the open end of the paper bag and scrunch the end of the bag around the tube. Wrap a long piece of tape in a spiral to secure the horse's head. The bag should fall forward. Children use markers or cut construction paper to make horse eyes, a nose and a mouth. A two by three inch rectangle of construction paper can be cut diagonally to make ears. For special effects, children may want to glue on a yarn mane or reins. Giddyup!

JANUARY

CYLINDER SCULPTURE

YOU WILL NEED:
    cardboard tubes of assorted sizes
    masking tape
    paintbrush
    tempera paint
    large piece of cardboard: approximately 12 by 18 inches (The top or
        side of a cardboard box is good.)

Assist children in attaching the cylinders vertically to the cardboard using as much masking tape as necessary. For an interesting effect, they may want to tape some rolls horizontally. Children may paint the town as desired.

FEBRUARY ♥

COOKIE DECORATING

Decorating cookies is a popular activity with children of all ages. Cut shapes that are appropriate for an upcoming holiday or for the season—hearts for Valentine's Day, chicks and bunnies for spring, stars for Independence Day. When working with a large group of children, use small paper cups to hold frosting and use craft sticks for spreading. Put an assortment of sprinkles in the cups of half an egg carton.

SUGAR COOKIES

Mix together flour, salt, baking powder and nutmeg. Cream shortening and sugar in a separate bowl. Add eggs and beat until fluffy. Add dry ingredients and milk alternately to shortening and sugar mixture, beating after each addition. Refrigerate. Roll out dough and assist children in cutting the shapes. Bake at 375° for five minutes on an ungreased cookie sheet. This recipe makes approximately one hundred cookies.

INGREDIENTS

1 1/4 cup shortening
 (part butter)
2 cups sugar
2 eggs
5 cups flour
4 tsp. baking powder
1 tsp. salt
1 tsp. nutmeg
1/2 cup milk

BASIC FROSTING

Mix all ingredients together. Add food coloring if desired.

INGREDIENTS

1 lb. confectioners'
 sugar
1/2 cup shortening
5 tbs. water
1 tsp. vanilla

 # FEBRUARY

MURAL PAINTING

YOU WILL NEED:
   large roll of paper: brown, butcher or shelf
   paint
   brushes

Roll out a long length of paper on the floor. Let each child select a work space on the paper and begin painting. When the murals are finished and dry, hang them up for everyone to admire.

FEBRUARY ♥

TEXTURE COLLAGE

YOU WILL NEED:
  glue
  heavy backing (e.g. Styrofoam
    tray, poster board, cardboard)
  assortment of materials: cotton
    or wool fabric, wood, nuts, seeds,
    sandpaper, rug remnants,
    aluminum foil, etc.

Children glue a variety of objects to
a sturdy backing. They may want
to close their eyes, touch, and
guess what the object is!

WOOD SCULPTURE

YOU WILL NEED:
  wood scraps
  glue
  flat base

Children firmly glue wood scraps to
a flat wooden base. They will need
to hold the scraps in place until
set. After the sculpture is firmly set,
children may paint it. (This should
probably be done on another day.)

♥ FEBRUARY

VALENTINE MAILBOX

YOU WILL NEED:
  two 9-inch paper plates
  piece of yarn, 1 yard long with one end taped or dipped in glue and
    dried to form a "needle"
  stapler
  hole punch
  markers, paper doilies, stickers
  glue

This fun project requires preparation beforehand. Cut a paper plate in half. Staple the half to a whole plate, right sides together, making a pocket. Punch holes two inches apart around the circumference and one half inch from the edge. Tie the yarn through a hole at the top. Children may lace around the edges. Tie the end to the starting point. A loop will remain to use as a hanger. Children may decorate to their hearts' content!

FEBRUARY ♥

VALENTINE CARD

YOU WILL NEED:
  red construction paper
  white paper doilies
  red, white, and pink ribbon
  Styrofoam popcorn
  glue

Assist children in folding construction paper in half. They may glue ribbon, snips of doilies, and Styrofoam popcorn to the front. Each child may give this special card to a favorite valentine.

19

 **FEBRUARY**

BOX FUN

YOU WILL NEED:
  boxes and cartons of assorted sizes
  decorating materials (e.g. paint, markers, crayons, construction paper,
    scissors, glue)

Discuss with children how a box can become anything one wishes. Tell them to decorate a box to create a bedroom for a stuffed animal, a crib for a doll, or a garage for a car. Appliance boxes become clubhouses, cartons become canoes, and shoe boxes become zoo cages. Children may camouflage a moon base, cut arm and leg holes for a turtle shell, or add burners and dials to make a stove. They may cut construction paper for windows, doors, hearts or flowers.

MARCH FLYER

YOU WILL NEED:
  small paper plate or heavy paper circle with 5-inch diameter
  glue
  5 or more strips of crepe paper, 12 inches long
  24-inch piece of string

Make a knot in one end of the string and thread it through a small hole in the center of the plate. Now make a knot against the other side of the plate. The flyer will be secure between the two knots. Children glue streamers around the circumference of the plate. Using the free end of the string as a handle, children may run with their flyers to catch the March wind.

 # MARCH

EGG CARTON PROJECTS

One egg carton can be used for the following projects. Styrofoam cartons are recommended so that children can do some of the cutting.

YOU WILL NEED:

egg carton	markers
construction paper	scissors
pipe cleaners	small bell
glue	yarn
yellow chalk	

CATERPILLAR

Discard the top of the egg carton. Assist children in cutting the carton lengthwise. They can make a caterpillar from one half by adding pipe cleaner antennae, construction paper eyes, and additional decorations.

MARCH

BELL

Children can cut half of an egg carton into single sections. Assist them in pushing a pipe cleaner through the bottom of the cup. Make a clapper by threading a real bell on the end of the pipe cleaner. Twist the end of the pipe cleaner to secure the bell inside the cup.

CHICK

Children can rub yellow chalk on a cotton ball and glue the cotton ball into the "egg shell" (carton section). They cut a tiny diamond shape from orange construction paper and fold the diamond in half to make a beak. Then, they glue it to the cotton ball and add eyes above the beak with a black marker.

FLOWER

Push a pipe cleaner up through the bottom center of the egg carton cup. Bend the end of the pipe cleaner to form a "knot." Pull the knot down into the cup forming the center of the flower. Children can make several cuts around the edge toward the center to form petals for the flower. Twisting the stems of several flowers together creates a bouquet.

# MARCH

PUSSY WILLOWS

YOU WILL NEED:
    construction paper
    glue
    marker
    cotton swabs

Draw free form lines on construction paper with a marker. Children can break swabs in half and glue them along the lines for the first sign of spring.

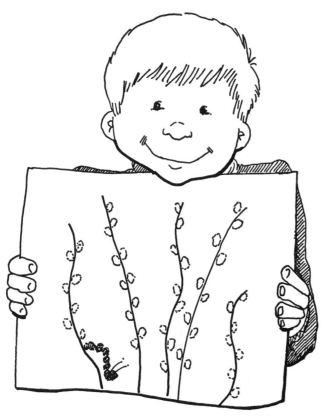

YOU WILL NEED:
    white paint
    colored construction paper
    marker

Children press their thumbs in paint and make prints along a free-form line to create pussy willows.

Thumb prints can make birds or can be strung together to make caterpillars.

FORSYTHIA

YOU WILL NEED:
 sponge
 yellow tempera paint
 construction paper
 marker

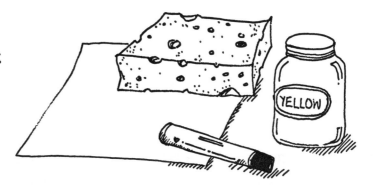

Help children cut or tear the sponge into small manageable pieces. Children then lightly dip the pieces into yellow tempera paint and print forsythia blossoms on construction paper. They can add stems to complete a spring bouquet. Later in the season, lavender paint can be used to make lilacs.

# MARCH

COOKIE CUTTER PUPPET

YOU WILL NEED:
  metal cookie cutters
  construction paper
  craft sticks
  glue
  assorted materials (cotton balls, rickrack, buttons, ribbon)
  markers

This project requires advance preparation, but the end result provides lots of imaginative play. To make puppets, use a dark marker to outline the cookie cutter on a piece of construction paper. Draw a square or rectangle around the shape. Even children who are just learning to use scissors can cut the straight lines. After the shape is cut out, children may glue a craft stick to the lower back for a handle. Children may want to use markers and assorted materials to decorate their puppets. A dinosaur could be covered with torn paper scales or a lamb could be covered with cotton balls. Trim a gingerbread figure with three buttons and yarn hair.

26

MILK CARTON PLANTERS

YOU WILL NEED:
  half pint milk or juice carton
  potting soil
  grass seed
  construction paper
  scissors
  crayons
  glue

Cut and remove the peak of the carton, leaving a square container. Children may cut a piece of construction paper to fit one side of the planter. Have them draw a face on the paper and glue it to the carton. Then, they fill the container with potting soil and plant grass seed accordingly. Placed in a sunny spot and watered regularly, Harry will soon sprout hair. He might need an occasional haircut, too!

 # APRIL

TORN PAPER PROJECTS

YOU WILL NEED:
  construction paper of assorted colors
  glue
  paper plates
  paper lunch bag
  newspaper
  yarn

Give students strips of paper to tear into small pieces. Have the children overlap and glue the pieces to give the effect of feathers or scales. Beginners might like tearing larger pieces to make a multicolored collage.

After putting a feathered or scaly friend together, children can use markers to add details such as beaks, feet, fins or tails.

Draw the outline of a chick and let the children fill it in with yellow "feathers" made by tearing paper.

A row of green overlapping "scales" can be a grass snake; a circle of "scales" can be a turtle.

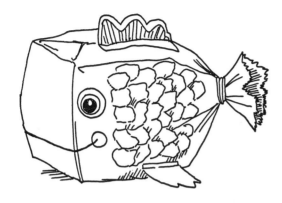

Have children stuff a paper lunch bag, secure the top, and add scales and fins for the catch of the day.

Have children turn a paper plate over and draw a face in the middle. Children may circle the face with an armadillo's armor, an eagle's ruff, or a fish's scales.

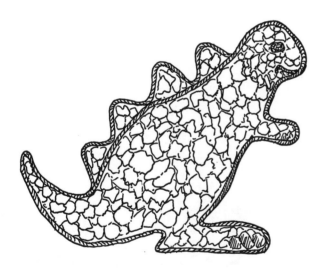

A free form dinosaur can be outlined by dipping yarn in glue and surrounding the creature. When the scales and outline have dried, children may "shine up" the scales by painting them with glue.

Torn paper projects are fun and easy. Artists may invent their own animals or fill in an outline. The projects will always be colorful and interesting.

 # APRIL

THEME COLLAGE

YOU WILL NEED:
    construction paper
    old magazines or catalogs
    scissors
    glue

Choose a theme such as toys, babies, or flowers. Children may cut or tear pictures from magazines, circulars, or catalogs. Have them glue the pictures to construction paper. Several pages may be combined for **a** child's book.

PIPE CLEANER PETS

TISSUE PAPER BUTTERFLY

YOU WILL NEED:
  20 by 30 inch piece of
    tissue paper
  pipe cleaner
  thinned tempera paint
  paintbrush or toothbrush

Have children spatter paint on tissue paper and let it dry. Help them gather the paper in the middle and tie it with the center of a pipe cleaner. To form the butterfly's antennae, children may fold and twist the tips of the pipe cleaner.

FUZZY SPIDER

YOU WILL NEED:
  4 pipe cleaners

Assist children in folding the four pipe cleaners in half and twisting them in the center. Extend and bend the ends for legs. The twisted top becomes the body.

APRIL

PAPER BAG COSTUME

AN ASTRONAUT

YOU WILL NEED:
  paper grocery bag
  construction paper
  tape
  scissors
  markers

Remove a face-sized section near the bottom of one wide side of a paper bag. Cut one hole in each narrow side, even with the face hole, to increase visibility. Invert the bag and have the astronaut try on the costume. Remove the costume and cut armholes. Air tanks may be added. Each tank is made by taping together the short ends of an 8 1/2 by 11 inch piece of paper to form a cylinder. Tape both tanks to the back of the bag. Children might like to use markers to draw stars and stripes and the NASA insignia. Blast off!

This paper bag costume can be modified to make other costumes. Children may want to make a knight in shining armor or a robot.

BASKET WEAVING

YOU WILL NEED:
  plastic berry basket
  yarn or ribbon
  tape

Cut pieces of yarn or ribbon in twenty-four-inch lengths. Wrap one end with tape to make a thin, pliable "needle." Tie the raw end to the basket. Children then weave in and out through the holes. A variety of colors gives a festive effect. Children may wish to add a handle or fill the basket with dandelions or violets.

 MAY

HAND PRINT CARD

YOU WILL NEED:
   construction paper
   marker
   crayons

Outline a child's hand on construction paper. Children may want to add a poem or special thought. This card makes a nice gift for Mother's Day.

VASES

YOU WILL NEED:
  sturdy plastic cup
  fabric scraps
  glue

  or:
  small jar, such as olive, baby food
    or pickle jar
  thinned tempera paint

Have children glue fabric scraps on a cup. When filled with flowers, this vase makes a festive Mother's Day gift.

Have children paint jars as they wish. Fresh or paper flowers add a special touch.

TREASURE BOX

YOU WILL NEED:
    sturdy box with a cover such as cigar, candy or shoe box
    collage materials such as paper, shells, string, yarn, fabric, buttons,
        ribbons, lace, pasta, foil, child's photo, magazine pictures, torn
        paper, feathers, Styrofoam popcorn, junk jewelry
    tissue paper or construction paper
    glue

Assist children in covering the box with tissue paper or construction paper.
Children may glue on collage materials to depict a theme or to make a
free-form design. Special treasures can be kept inside.

CROWN

YOU WILL NEED:
   8 1/2 by 11 inch construction paper
   stapler
   glue
   decorations of your choice: pieces of foil, tissue paper, paper doilies

Have children draw a zigzag line through the middle of the construction paper and cut along the line. Then help them staple the two parts together to form one long strip. Children should decorate the paper while flat. Wrap the crown around the child's head to measure for fit. Remove the crown and staple both ends together in the appropriate places. Crown your students king and queen.

JUNE

MUSICAL INSTRUMENTS

TAMBOURINE

YOU WILL NEED:
    2 paper plates
    stapler or masking tape
    dry macaroni
    crepe paper and
        glue (optional)

Place dry macaroni between two paper plates, right sides together. Staple or tape the plates together. Children may add crepe paper streamers or other decorations. They will enjoy shaking or banging their tambourines. Let the parade begin.

SANDPAPER BLOCKS

YOU WILL NEED:
    smooth scrap wood
        blocks
    sandpaper
    glue

Have children glue sandpaper to the blocks and let them dry. They can clap or rub the wood blocks together. March on!

JUNE

DRUM

YOU WILL NEED:
  heavy-duty box with a lid, such as
    a gift or oatmeal box
  craft sticks or other drumsticks
  hole punch
  string or yarn
  additional decorations (optional)

KAZOO

YOU WILL NEED:
  cardboard tube, 6 inches long
  piece of wax paper, 6 inches
    square
  masking tape

Assist children in placing wax paper over one end of the tube and taping it securely. Holding the kazoo against their lips, children can hum a happy tune.

Remove the lid from the box. With a hole punch, make a hole in opposite sides of the box near the top. Tie a thirty-inch piece of string through the holes. Replace the lid. Children may decorate their drums if they wish and then bang to beat the band!

JUNE

FINGER PAINTING

Finger painting is a good indoor and outdoor activity. An uncluttered floor space is helpful. Keep a pan of water nearby for washing hands. Heavy shelf paper can be used or you may purchase finger paint paper from craft stores. The enjoyment children receive from this activity is well worth the cleanup involved.

FINGER PAINT RECIPE

YOU WILL NEED:
  1 cup flour
  2 cups cold water
  1 tsp. salt
  2 cups hot water
  food coloring or tempera paint

Mix flour, salt and cold water in a saucepan to make a smooth paste. Add hot water and cook over medium heat until the mixture thickens and changes from white to a darker color. Remove from heat. Add food coloring or tempera paint. (Wintergreen or vanilla flavoring may be added to reduce the flour odor.) To create interesting textures, add sand, sawdust, or coffee grounds. The finger paint is usable for one week. It will mold if kept longer.

PENCIL HOLDER

YOU WILL NEED:
  empty juice can
  construction paper
  tape
  markers
  scissors

Check the opening of a clean, empty juice can for sharp edges. Then, cut a piece of construction paper one inch larger than the height and circumference of the container. Align the paper with the bottom edge of the can. Tape one end of the paper along the side. Roll the can up in the paper and tape securely. Tuck the paper hem into the top opening. Children can decorate their cans with markers. With an added pencil or two, this is a perfect Father's Day gift.

COFFEE CAN BANK

YOU WILL NEED:
  empty coffee can and
    plastic lid
  construction paper
  tape
  markers
  scissors

Remove the plastic lid. Cut a slot large enough for a coin in the center. Cutting the paper the same height as the can, follow the same procedure used to cover the pencil holder. Put the lid back on the can. Children may decorate the can and then keep their pennies inside.

☀ JUNE

ROCK PAPERWEIGHT

YOU WILL NEED:
   scissors
   fist-size rock
   glue
   Styrofoam tray or
      similar container (for glue)
   printed paper napkin
      of good quality

Have children wash and dry a favorite rock. Make a solution with equal parts of water and glue. Children then fully open the napkin and immerse it in the glue. After carefully removing this gooey napkin, they press it around the rock, smoothing out the wrinkles as they go. Have them trim off any excess napkin. When completely dry, the paperweight makes a nice Father's Day gift.

PAPER HOLDER

YOU WILL NEED:
   fist-size rock
   glue
   clothespin
   pasta shells or seashells

Children should wash and dry their rocks. Then have them glue the flat side of the clothespin onto the rock and let it dry completely. They will like decorating their paper holders with pasta shapes or seashells. As a special touch, a name can be spelled in pasta letters. Children can clip on a special card or photo.

42

JUNE

BINOCULARS

YOU WILL NEED:
   2 cardboard tubes, 6 inches
      long
   masking tape
   twenty-four-inch piece of string
   hole punch
   markers
   colored cellophane (optional)

Tape two tubes together, side by side. If you want to add a strap, punch a hole in each side of the binoculars and run a twenty-four-inch piece of string through each hole. Children may want to add colored cellophane lenses, camouflage, or other decorations.

SPYGLASS

YOU WILL NEED:
   2 empty paper towel tubes
   masking tape
   markers or paint

Circle the middle of one tube with marker or tape. Squeeze one half of the tube so that it will fit into the second tube. Children can extend their spyglasses, but should not pull the scope beyond the marked circle. They may want to add paint or marker decorations.

 # JULY

DIP AND DRIP PAINTING

YOU WILL NEED:
    small containers, such as coffee cups
    white or pastel paper towels, tissue paper, or other absorbent paper
    food coloring
    craft sticks or cotton swabs
    water

Put one half cup water in each of three small containers. Add ten drops of red food coloring to one container, ten drops of blue to the second, and ten drops of yellow to the third. Children can dip a craft stick in one of the containers and drip the colored water on the paper towel. Dipping and dripping makes a beautiful design in the primary colors. Children will discover how colors change when mixed.

NATURE COLLAGE

YOU WILL NEED:
  scrap wood for a base
  sandpaper
  blue or green tempera paint
  paintbrush
  shells, pine cones, stones, flowers, grass, or twigs
  glue

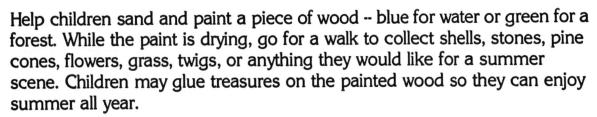

Help children sand and paint a piece of wood -- blue for water or green for a forest. While the paint is drying, go for a walk to collect shells, stones, pine cones, flowers, grass, twigs, or anything they would like for a summer scene. Children may glue treasures on the painted wood so they can enjoy summer all year.

 # JULY

NATURE RUBBINGS

YOU WILL NEED:
   light-colored construction paper
   chalk or jumbo crayon

Allow children to be in touch with the outdoors by having them close their eyes and feel tree bark, stones, ferns, or leaves. When they open their eyes, let them press a piece of construction paper against one of these surfaces and rub lightly with the side of a piece of chalk or a crayon. Children may want to try lots of different rubbings and then have a friend guess what they are.

JULY

FLAGS

YOU WILL NEED:
    cardboard tube (paper towel roll)
    8 1/2 by 11 inch construction paper
    markers
    star stickers
    tape

Have children decorate both sides of the paper. Star stickers may be added. Make a one-half-inch fold along one edge. To attach the flag to the flagpole, tape the folded edge of the paper to the tube. Reverse the flag and tape the back of the fold. Children may wave their flags to celebrate.

 # JULY

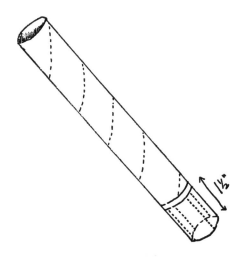

SPACESHIP

YOU WILL NEED:
   cardboard tube (paper towel roll)
   5-ounce paper cup
   masking tape
   markers

Encircle the tube with tape 1 1/2 inches from the end. Make four evenly spaced cuts below the tape. Children may stabilize their rocket bases by flaring the cut pieces outward. They may add the nose cone by inverting the cup over the base. Let children decorate their spaceships and blast off.

SUNFLOWERS

POTTED SUNFLOWERS

YOU WILL NEED:
  9-ounce paper cup
  potting soil
  sunflower seeds
  spoon
  water

Have children fill a nine-ounce paper cup with moistened potting soil and push three sunflower seeds into the soil. While waiting for their seeds to sprout, children can make paper cup sunflowers to add to their pots.

PAPER CUP SUNFLOWERS

YOU WILL NEED:
  scissors   cotton ball
  3-ounce paper cup   markers
  pipe cleaner   colored chalk

Cut a paper cup from the rim to the base several times. Fold each section outward, halfway down the cup. Make a small puncture for the pipe cleaner stem in the base of the cup. Children can insert the stem through the hole and then gently push the cotton into the center of the sunflower so the point of the pipe cleaner is covered. Children may color the petals and center with markers or colored chalk. Have them tape the stem to the outside of the flower pot.

49

AUGUST

BUBBLES AND BLOWERS

YOU WILL NEED:
  1 gallon water
  1 cup mild liquid detergent
  plastic dishpan
  juice can with both ends removed
  plastic berry basket

Put one gallon of water in the dishpan. Add one cup of liquid detergent. Have children dip a juice can in the solution and then blow gently against the bubble film to make a gigantic bubble. They may dip one or two berry baskets and swirl them through the air to leave a trail of bubbles.

AUGUST

TOY BOAT

YOU WILL NEED:
   16-ounce or smaller plastic container with lid (margarine or ice cream container)
   2 craft sticks
   masking tape
   vinyl tape
   aluminum foil
   clay

Boat:

Make a slit in the center of the lid. Children can press a small ball of clay against the bottom center of the container. Replace the lid and let children decorate it with vinyl tape.

Sail:

Take a twelve-inch square of foil and fold it in half twice to form a six-inch square.

Mast:

Overlap the craft sticks one inch and tape them together.

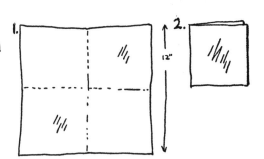

Putting it all together:

Starting at one corner, roll the foil around the end of the mast until you reach the center of the square. This leaves a triangular sail.

Insert the mast through the slit of the lid and anchor the end of the mast in the clay.

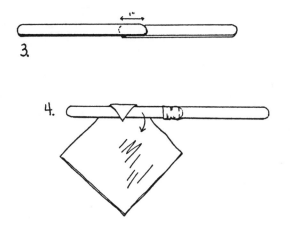

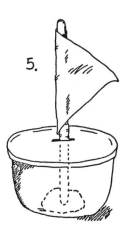

Note: This activity requires some adult preparation, but children enjoy decorating their boats and "sailing away" in a tub or wading pool.

⛵ AUGUST

PRINTING

YOU WILL NEED:
  newsprint, construction
    paper, tissue paper, or
    butcher paper
  Styrofoam trays
  sponges
  thinned tempera paint
  household utensils such as:
    wire whisk,
    meat mallet,
    fork,
    plastic lid,
    string,
    cookie cutter,
    potato masher,
    spatula

vegetables or fruits
  cut in half such as:
  potato,
  apple,
  orange,
  green pepper,
  mushroom,
  carrot
washable toys such as:
  alphabet blocks or
  plastic building blocks

Note: You may be able to
purchase inexpensive end
rolls of newsprint from your
local newspaper.

AUGUST

Use a separate tray and sponge for each color. Place the sponge on the tray and saturate it with tempera paint. Leave the sponge on the tray. Children then select an object, press it into the sponge, and print. They may want to try different shapes and sizes. When more paint is needed, flip the sponge over. Children may want to use the last bits of paint by printing with the sponge. Display and admire the printing or let children use it as wrapping paper.

AUGUST

PAINT PLAY

WATER PAINTING

YOU WILL NEED:
   empty container
   water
   paintbrush

Have children fill their containers with water. Give the children brushes and watch them paint the outside world with imaginary colors.

ROCK PAINTING

YOU WILL NEED:
   rock
   tempera paint
   brush

After washing and drying the rocks, children will enjoy painting original designs on them. When dry, the rock makes a nice paperweight.

DECORATIVE BOTTLE

YOU WILL NEED:
   empty liquid detergent or
     baby shampoo bottle
   colored vinyl tape

Wash the container thoroughly. Children may decorate it with vinyl tape. After filling it with water, they will enjoy watering plants, making mud pies, or even spraying themselves to keep cool!

AUGUST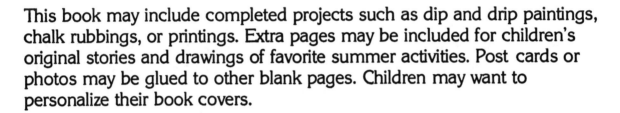

SUMMER SCRAPBOOK

YOU WILL NEED:
    thin cardboard or oak tag
    hole punch
    string or yarn
    light-colored construction paper
    paper projects completed during the summer
    pencil, crayons, markers
    glue

This book may include completed projects such as dip and drip paintings, chalk rubbings, or printings. Extra pages may be included for children's original stories and drawings of favorite summer activities. Post cards or photos may be glued to other blank pages. Children may want to personalize their book covers.

Punch two or three holes along the side of each page, including the front and back covers. Lace the pages together with string or yarn and tie the ends securely.

SEPTEMBER

PROJECT ENVELOPE

YOU WILL NEED:
   18 by 24 inch piece of oak tag
   stickers
   markers
   stapler or masking tape
   scissors

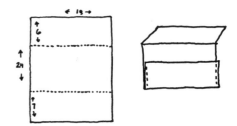

Lay the oak tag vertically. Fold the lower edge up seven inches and crease it. Tape or staple the sides to make a pocket. Fold the top of the oak tag down six inches to form a flap for the envelope. Crease the fold and round the edges of the flap. Children will enjoy decorating their envelopes with markers and stickers. They can fill the envelopes with wonderful projects.

SEPTEMBER

MILK CARTON SCHOOL BUS

YOU WILL NEED:
  clean, empty milk carton (quart or half gallon size)
  construction paper
  tape
  glue
  scissors

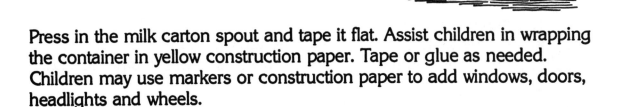

Press in the milk carton spout and tape it flat. Assist children in wrapping the container in yellow construction paper. Tape or glue as needed. Children may use markers or construction paper to add windows, doors, headlights and wheels.

Children may want to cover and decorate cartons of various sizes to form a train or a truck fleet.

 # SEPTEMBER

MANUAL TRAFFIC SIGN

YOU WILL NEED:
- construction paper
- glue
- craft sticks
- scissors
- masking tape

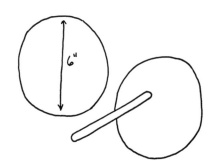

Trace one green and one red circle of six-inch diameter. Children can cut them out. Tape the craft stick between the circles and let children glue them together. They can flip the sign from one side to the other to play "Stop and Go."

Children might like to make a traffic light by gluing circles of red, green and yellow on a darker background.

SEPTEMBER

SAFETY OFFICER'S BADGE

YOU WILL NEED:
   cardboard
   foil
   star stickers
   construction paper
   masking tape
   scissors

Have children cut a triangle from cardboard. Help them round off the corners and cover the "badge" with foil. They can add star stickers or construction paper cutouts. Attach masking tape rolled in a circle to the back of the badge. Children will wear them proudly.

WALKIE-TALKIE

YOU WILL NEED:
   empty juice box or single-
      serving cereal box
   construction paper
   tape
   markers
   11-inch straw

Assist children in covering a small cardboard box with construction paper. They can add a straw to the top for an antenna and draw a speaker and two control knobs on the box.

 # SEPTEMBER

FIREFIGHTER'S HAT

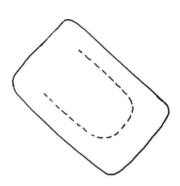

YOU WILL NEED:
 red and white construction paper
 scissors
 glue
 markers

Round off the corners of a sheet of red 8 1/2 by 11 inch construction paper. Draw a horseshoe-shaped line within the length of the paper, leaving a margin of 2 1/2 inches on the ends and 1 1/2 inches on the sides. Cut along the line creating a U-shaped flap. Children can add a badge to the uncut edge of the horseshoe. When placed on the head, the flap becomes the front of the firefighter's hat.

PAINTED LEAVES, PRINTED LEAVES

YOU WILL NEED:
  tempera paint
  paintbrush
  leaves
  paper
  newsprint, construction paper, or paper towels
  clear Contact paper (optional)

Painted

Have children paint leaves with one or more colors. After they are dry, the children may seal them between two pieces of Contact paper. Display these for all to admire.

Printed

To make leaf prints on paper, thoroughly paint or dip leaves and press them against newsprint, construction paper or paper towels. Children may peel away the leaves to discover
pretty autumn scenes.

OCTOBER

AUTUMN ARRANGEMENT

YOU WILL NEED:
    small container
    modeling clay
    dried weeds, leaves or flowers

Have children fill a small container with modeling clay. After gathering dried leaves, weeds, and flowers, help them arrange a fall bouquet by pushing the stems into the clay.

OCTOBER

FALL COLLAGE

YOU WILL NEED:
  backing material
    (Styrofoam trays, sturdy
    paper plates or cardboard)
  leaves, pine cones, dried
    flowers and grass
  several kinds of seeds
  yarn

Take a nature walk to collect
materials for gluing and weaving.
Children can glue their treasures to
a sturdy backing for a collage.

GRASS WEAVING

YOU WILL NEED:
  backing material
    (Styrofoam trays, sturdy
    paper plates or cardboard)
  leaves, pine cones, dried
    flowers and grass
  several kinds of seeds
  yarn

Children create the weaving by
winding yarn five or six times
around a backing which has been
notched to keep the yarn from
slipping. Tie the ends of the yarn
together in the back. Children then
weave dried grass over and under
the yarn. They may add pine cones
and flowers. Display their creations
in a special place.

OCTOBER

TRICK OR TREAT BAG

YOU WILL NEED:
  paper lunch bag
  orange and black construction
    paper
  glue
  markers

Children will enjoy drawing and
gluing Halloween decorations on a
paper bag. Orange and black
paper scraps can be very
decorative. Specific designs are not
necessary. It will be a treat for children
to use their bags on Halloween.

LOLLIPOP GHOST PUPPET

YOU WILL NEED:
  facial tissue
  lollipop
  yarn
  markers

Assist children in covering a
lollipop with a facial tissue and
tying a piece of yarn below the
candy. Children can add a face
with markers. When tired of their
ghosts, they can eat them.

OCTOBER

PAPER PLATE MASKS

YOU WILL NEED:
  paper plates
  yarn
  markers
  scissors
  stapler
  glue
  paper scraps
  assorted materials
  hole punch

Cut away all or part of the inner circle of a paper plate, leaving plenty of room for eyes. (If you leave a strip across the middle, it will give some strength to the paper plate.) Tie yarn or string through holes punched on each side of the plate. Children can decorate their masks with markers, construction paper, crepe paper, scraps of cloth or felt, Mylar film, wood shavings, ribbon, old jewelry, cotton, fake fur, feathers, and anything else!

OCTOBER

Make a clown with yarn hair.

Create a lamb with fuzzy cotton ball fleece.

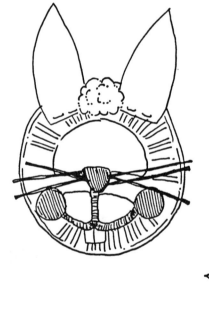

Decorate a rabbit mask with stapled ears.

Make a bird with a cone-shaped paper cup beak and feathers.

OCTOBER

PUMPKIN PROJECT

YOU WILL NEED:
  a pumpkin
  scissors
  masking tape
  your choice of: paint, markers, wood shavings, Mylar, cotton balls,
    corn husks or silks, vegetable pieces, construction paper
  glue

Children can decorate a real pumpkin with paint, markers, or finger paints.
If they would like to change the pumpkin's face, they may wash off the
paint and start again. They may add a little character with decorations of
their choice.

 NOVEMBER

PAPER BAG TURKEY

YOU WILL NEED:
   paper lunch bag
   newspaper
   construction paper
   markers or paint
   string or yarn
   tape
   scissors
   feathers (optional)

Have children stuff a lunch bag with crumpled newspaper. Make sure they leave enough space to close the bag and tie a piece of string tightly around it. (The tied end is the turkey's head.) Children can make a tail by gluing or taping feathers, cut from several colors of paper, to the opposite end of the bag. They may use markers to give the turkey eyes, a beak and more feathers.

You may want to make a paper head that can be glued onto the bag.

fold in ½

& glue!

NOVEMBER

INDIAN HEADBAND

YOU WILL NEED:
    butcher paper or paper bag
    construction paper and/or feathers
    stapler
    markers
    scissors

Cut a strip of butcher paper five inches wide and an inch or two longer than the circumference of the child's head. Fold it in half lengthwise. Staple it near the open edge at two inch intervals.

Overlap the ends so the band fits the child's head snugly and staple the band securely.

Children can cut feathers six to eight inches in length from several colors of construction paper. (They may add real feathers if they wish.) They may draw Indian designs and geometric designs on the band and/or the paper feathers. Assist children in slipping the feathers into the open edge of the band between the staples. Children can leave the feathers loose and rearrange them occasionally, or they may staple them.

NOVEMBER

PLACE CARD

YOU WILL NEED:
    3 by 5 inch recipe cards
    glue
    marker
    poultry seasoning
    dried flowers or seeds
        (optional)

Have children fold a card in half.
Leaving space for their name, they
should smear glue on the card and
sprinkle it with poultry seasoning.
After shaking off excess seasoning,
they may glue on flowers or seeds
as desired. The name may then be
added.

PLACE MAT

YOU WILL NEED:
    construction paper
    stickers
    markers
    clear Contact paper or
        laminating film

Children can decorate an 8 1/2 by
11 inch piece of construction
paper with markers and stickers.
Help them seal it between two
pieces of clear Contact paper or
laminate it.

NOVEMBER

TURKEY HAND PRINT

YOU WILL NEED:
  paper
  markers or crayons
  feathers (optional)
  glue
  scissors

Place the child's hand, with fingers spread apart, on a piece of paper and trace around it. (The thumb becomes the turkey's head, and the fingers become feathers.) Children may glue on real feathers or color in bright feathers with markers. They may add paper feet and a beak to make their turkeys complete.

PAPER PLATE TURKEY

YOU WILL NEED:
  paper plate
  construction paper
  scissors
  glue

Have children glue cut or torn construction paper feathers around a portion of the paper plate. After adding a head and feet, they will have a plate for Thanksgiving dinner.

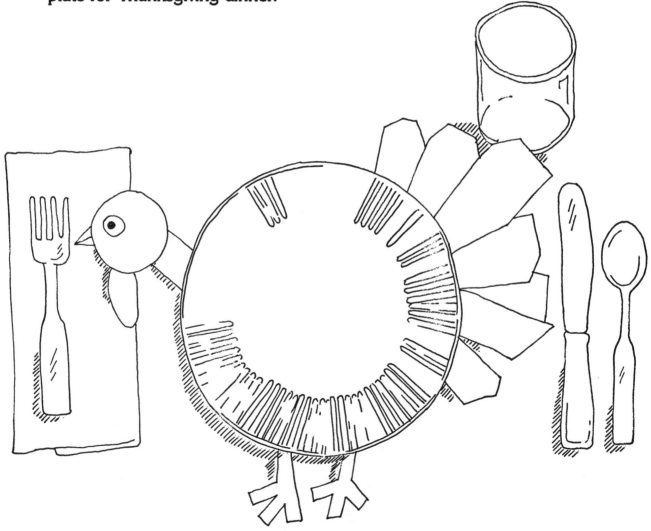

NOVEMBER

STRUNG NECKLACE

YOU WILL NEED:
  string or yarn
  assorted items to string

Cut an eighteen-inch piece of string or yarn. Dip one end in glue diluted with water and then let it dry to form a "needle." Tie the other end of the yarn around the first item you string. Children may thread the various items and then join the ends to form a necklace.

SOAP SCULPTURE

YOU WILL NEED:
   1 cup soap granules
   1/2 cup water
   dark construction paper

Pour the soap granules into a large bowl. Gradually add water and whip with a wire whisk. When the mixture is thick and fluffy, children can smear or sculpt a wintry scene on dark construction paper.

DECEMBER ☆

CARDBOARD OR STRING SNOWFLAKE

YOU WILL NEED:
  dark construction paper
  white tempera paint
  cardboard 4 inches wide or
    string 6 inches long
  Styrofoam tray

Pour a small amount of paint in a Styrofoam tray. Have children hold one end of the string in each hand and dip the center part in the paint. With the string taut, they press it against the paper. Children then rotate the string 60° and press again. After rotating another 60° and pressing, the three lines should intersect in the center and form a snowflake. The same result can be achieved by using the edge of a piece of cardboard instead of the string.

WINTER MURAL

YOU WILL NEED:
  dark construction paper
  chalk
  cotton balls or batting
  glue

Children can create a winter storm by drawing chalk snowflakes and by gluing cotton clouds on dark construction paper.

# ☆ DECEMBER

SNOWMAN

YOU WILL NEED:
  dark construction paper
  marker
  glue
  cotton balls, popped popcorn, or Styrofoam packing material

Draw the outline of a snowman on a piece of construction paper. Children can glue on cotton balls, popcorn, or Styrofoam packing material. They may wish to add snowflakes to complete the picture.

DECEMBER ☆

DECORATIVE HANGINGS

PAPER PLATE PICTURE FRAME

YOU WILL NEED:
- a favorite photo
- 2 paper plates
- glue
- tissue or crepe paper cut in 2-inch squares
- yarn, string or ribbon
- scissors
- hole punch

Have children glue a favorite photo in the center of a paper plate. Attach a loop of yarn to the top of the plate. In the center of the second plate, cut a hole the size of the photo. To decorate the frame, children may bunch up pieces of tissue or crepe paper and glue them around the outside edge of the second plate. Children then glue the plates together.

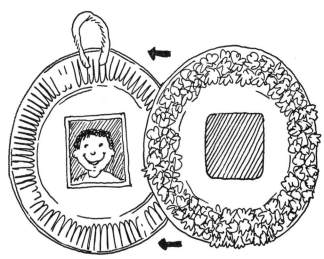

LIGHT CATCHER

YOU WILL NEED:
- clear plastic lid
- colored cellophane
- yarn or ribbon
- glue
- hole punch

Children may glue colored cellophane on one or both sides of a clear plastic lid. Use a hole punch to make a hole for the yarn or ribbon hanger.

# DECEMBER

SELF-PORTRAIT

YOU WILL NEED:
    30 inch by 48 inch piece of paper
    markers or paint
    scissors
    fabric scraps, buttons, yarn, etc.

Have the child lie face-up on the paper. After tracing the child's outline, let the child decorate the self-portrait. Children may want to glue on yarn to make hair, buttons to decorate shirts, and Velcro to attach shoes.

DECEMBER ☆

PAPER BAG REINDEER PUPPET

YOU WILL NEED:
 paper lunch bag
 construction paper
 glue
 scissors
 markers

The reindeer puppet opens his mouth to talk when the child puts a hand into the bag and curves fingers around the flap created by the flattened bottom. The child may draw or glue eyes, ears and a nose on the flap. Outline the child's wrists and hands on construction paper and cut along the lines. Have the child glue the "hands" to the back of the bag for antlers.